THE ANGRY TOOLBOX ADVENTURES

Written by Mike J.B.

Illustrated by Gemma Stanley

www.angry-toolbox.com

Grosvenor House
Publishing Limited

This book is published by
Grosvenor House Publishing Ltd
Link House
140 The Broadway, Tolworth, Surrey, KT6 7HT.
www.grosvenorhousepublishing.co.uk

A CIP record for this book
is available from the British Library

Paperback ISBN 978-1-83615-072-5
Hardback ISBN 978-1-83615-068-8

Dedication from the Author

"Thank you to Leroy and his toolbox,
for this new adventure, and carrying on the journey."

Mike J.B.

Dedication from the illustrator

"For my little ladies, my inspiration and my muses."

Gemma Stanley

Chapter 1

A New Dawn

It was the end of the festive season and a New Year was in sight for the Boulder family. As Leroy ventured downstairs, he passed his mum and dad, who were busily removing the Christmas decorations throughout the house. Leroy's dad was removing the batteries from the twinkling fairy lights and Mum was carefully packaging each bauble from the tree. Grandad Boulder was sitting quietly in his chair by the window, almost asleep, glancing at the snow-covered reindeer, polar bear, and snowmen decorations still on the front lawn.

"Morning," called Leroy as he passed his mum and dad. "Morning, Grandad. Is it still icy outside?" he asked as he passed the window. Then he asked

excitedly, "Can I go to the basement?" He had missed his toolbox over the last few days while the family had been out for the Christmas festivities.

"Yes, but be careful down there," replied Mum. Before Mum had finished, Leroy had reached the other side of the hallway and had his hand on the handle to the door. He tried to open the door, but it was stiff and seemed stuck. He gave it another try and as he did, the door opened and the cold air hit him like a …

"Wow, that's freezing!" whispered Leroy as he shuddered. He started to venture down the stairs into the basement. The steps were covered in frost and Leroy was worried he was going to slip. As he descended into the basement, the air felt colder until he reached the bottom step, which was completely covered in frost. Leroy was confused. Why was the basement so cold and frosty? His eyes glanced towards the basement door at the far side, which was wide open.

Leroy remembered that Grandad Boulder had been down in the basement the day before, searching for some oil. He must have forgotten to close the door. Leroy walked over to the door and started to heave it shut. It was heavy and hard to push, as the hinges were frosty. But he closed it gently, mindful that the toolbox was sleeping. As the door clicked shut, the toolbox woke with a shiver.

"Brrr, brr, brrr." The toolbox shuddered as he felt the cold moist air in the basement. He tried to flick one eye open slowly, but it was stuck. "Flick, flick." He tried again but had no luck.

The toolbox began to moan. "Grrraaa," he hollered. He tried again. "Flick, flick." Slowly, he managed to half open one of his eyes and noticed tiny globules of ice gluing his eyelash together. "Finally," he shouted as he opened it fully and glanced around the basement. The toolbox was confused. As he looked around, he noticed that everything was covered in a white powdery substance. "Brrr, brrr." He shivered again as he carried on looking out of the only eye that was open. The floor, the benches, the shelves, and the old toolbox above were all covered in this strange white powder. He noticed Leroy standing in front of him.

"Good morning, Toolbox," said Leroy.

"Hello," grunted the toolbox.

"I am really sorry it is so cold and frosty in here today," Leroy began. "Grandad came down to the basement last night and he must have forgotten to close the door."

"Hmm…" the toolbox replied. "What is the white stuff, and where did it come from?"

"That's frost. I'll explain later," replied Leroy. "Grandad is very old and he can be forgetful sometimes. Dad tells me that as you get older, your brain doesn't work as quickly as before. You get slower and forget things."

"Oh dear. Well, it looks a bit different in here today, but we're all fine, so don't be cross with your grandad. We'll have to make sure we help him when he's in here," suggested the toolbox.

"Great idea" replied Leroy. "That would be really kind."

Just then Leroy's mum shouted from the top of the basement steps. It was time for breakfast and Leroy had to go.

* * *

The early morning sun had started to shine through the windows. The angry toolbox jumped as the sun warmed up the icy covering in the basement. Creak, crack, crack.

Beams of light were shining like lasers onto the shelves, enhancing the water droplets on stilts resembling sparkling diamonds. The toolbox started to flick his other eye a few times… flick, flick, flick until it finally opened. It felt sticky and gritty like the other eye for a while until it finally cleared and he could see. "Phew," he gasped. He continued looking around the basement. He looked up and down, towards the door to the house and over to the outside door. All was still apart from a noise from above.

He could hear a moan and a rattle. He looked up and realised it was coming from Grandad's old toolbox. He was trying to wake up but found his eyes were firmly stuck shut, and his moustache was like an icy rock. "Hello, old boy" called the angry toolbox.

"Mmmmm," was the reply. The old toolbox's lips and eyes were frozen. As he tried to force them open, he let out a loud yell. "Oh dear… FROST!"

"Oh, have you seen this before?" asked the toolbox.

"Yes, many times and a lot worse than this!" replied Grandad's old toolbox. "When I was in the field working on all the broken machines, it was cold, wet, freezing, icy, *and* frosty on many occasions."

The angry toolbox was eager to find out more, so Grandad's old toolbox began to explain. "Frost occurs when cold air and warm air collide. It creates a water vapour, which freezes and becomes a frosty icy covering. It disappears quite quickly on most occasions."

The angry toolbox was fascinated.

"Was the door left open to the outside?" he asked.

"Yes, it was," said the angry toolbox. "Leroy told us that his grandad had left it open last night."

Just then the toolboxes stopped talking, as they heard a strange sound from below.

"WHOOSH, WHOOSH, WHOOSH," went the noise.

The angry toolbox looked down and all around. He noticed as he did this that the side of his toolbox at the top was very icy, but at the bottom it was not. *Strange*, he thought as he carried on looking towards the area where the noise was coming from. He looked but could not see anything. He looked away, then again came the noise: "WHOOSH, WHOOSH, WHOOSH." But still he had no idea what it was, or where it was coming from.

Chapter 2

A Frosty, Icy Time

The angry toolbox looked again to see where the strange noise was coming from, but he was also concerned with getting his lid open to the fresh air so he could talk to his tools. But just like his eyes, his lid was stuck firm.

"Oh dear," he said. "My lid is truly stuck shut."

He tried with all his might to release it. He groaned, "ARH, ARH, EHH, EHH, RAH, RAH," as he used all his power to raise his frozen stuck lid – but with no success. The toolbox tried many times. He pushed, shoved, and heaved, but it was stuck fast.

Meanwhile, the old toolbox was watching and he smiled, with his moustache all covered in frost and icicles. Then he whispered, as he chuckled, "Many times in the past my lid was firmly stuck fast with ice and frost and it took a long time to become unfrozen. This was because we were outside more often than inside, not inside like this."

The angry toolbox asked, "But why were you outside?"

So the old toolbox started to explain. "I was an army issue toolbox and was working with Grandad Boulder outside. We lived in tents all the time because he was a soldier. And we repaired broken equipment." The old toolbox was getting louder as his lips were becoming unfrozen.

"How did the equipment get broken?" the angry toolbox asked.

"Well," said the old toolbox, "we were at WAR."

"War?" said the angry toolbox. "What is that?"

The old toolbox thought and pondered for a moment. "Hmm… hmm…" he groaned. "War," he said, "is when leaders of countries are nasty and unfriendly to others. Usually, it's because they want something that's not theirs. Or they just want to hurt each other, and all the people around them. So they call each other nasty names and shout and holler at each other."

"But I was angry and nasty and sad," said the angry toolbox. "And a bully."

"Yes," said the old toolbox, "but you changed before you hurt someone, unlike in a war situation. War leaves lots of people hurt and sad, but eventually it stops. It's pointless."

"Yes, I agree," said the angry toolbox. "Yes, it is pointless." Then he glanced up at the old toolbox, whose eyes remained semi-stuck shut with icicles still on his moustache. The angry toolbox wanted to get some fresh air in the toolbox. He pondered. Then a moment later he said, "Aha! Got it. I know what to do to help this situation. And he whispered, "Arne, Arne, Arne." But he got no response. Again, louder, he shouted, "Arne, Arne, Arne."

But in response he got nothing but a loud snoring from the old toolbox.

So he shouted more loudly still, "Arneee. Arneee."

"All of a sudden, a voice said, "Who's that?" It was Arne, who had woken up from the shouting. He spoke. "Is that you shouting, Angry?"

"Yes, it is," said the angry toolbox. "Sorry I woke you," he added.

"Hello – and morning," said Arne after a very large yawn.

The angry toolbox said, "I need your help."

Arne said, "What's up?"

The angry toolbox started to explain that his lid was stuck shut, and he could not open it, that it would not budge.

Arne shuffled in the dark and said, "Hmm... maybe I can assist." Then he stood up, flexed his big arms, shrugged his big shoulders and placed himself under the lid. Squatting down like a weightlifter, he said, "One, two, three." Then he grunted, "URH, URH, URH," as he pressed with all his strength. He gradually unbent and slowly straightened, creaking all around as he did, with pieces of frosty ice pinging off in all directions.

Suddenly, the lid went BANG as it flung open. Bang, bang, bang! The lid went from side to side, making the whole toolbox shake, rattle, and roll.

"WHOL!" came the sound from inside the toolbox as all the voices came to life, wondering what was going on.

"Sorry," said Arne and explained what was going on. As the rocking and rolling was settling down, he looked around.

"WHOL! What is with all the white icy stuff?" came the voice again.

The toolbox replied, saying that the cellar doors had been left open all night and the cold had come in, creating an icy covering over everything.

Arne leant over and touched the outside of the toolbox. "That's cold," he said. "And its blooming chilly." He looked around towards the window where the sun was just venturing through the icy covering. Creaks and cracking noises were being heard all the time. He glanced towards the basement floor. *Strange*, Arne thought as he noticed lots of shiny greyish lines in the frosty floor going around the benches.

All of a sudden came a "WHOOSH, WHOOSH" as Scribble whizzed past below.

"Oi," said Arne, but Scribble did not hear, or stop. Again, there was a "WHOOSH, WHOOSH" as Scribble passed by once more.

Arne shouted, "Oi, Scribble." This time Scribble stopped.

"Oh, hello Arne," he said.

Arne was curious. "What're you doing, Scribbs?" he asked.

"Out for a run," he said, "to keep warm as it's so frosty and cold today."

"Frosty," said Arne. "You bet. We used to come across this many times when we were with old Grandad in the field. Cold horrible icy frosty dew, caused when cold air and warm air collide, making this stuff form everywhere – and on everything."

Scribble replied, "Just doing a few laps to get the circulation moving. Think everyone should do it," he added.

"Hmm… maybe," Arne said. "We'll see. How do you know when to stop – when you're puffed out?"

"Nah," said Scribble, "when I go blunt."

"Blunt?" said Arne.

"Yes," said Scribble. "When my nib wears down, it slows me down, then I almost stop. So I have to creep back slowly like a sloth into the toolbox, have a rest, then find my sharpener, place myself in it and do a sort of twisting movement backwards and forwards. It's like doing the twist. After a while, hoorah, my nib is sharp again, like a dart ready for another day."

The angry toolbox, meanwhile, who was listening and looking down, said to Scribble, "How did *you* get out when *my* lid has been stuck shut with ice?"

"Ah," said Scribble, "well last night I was sitting outside relaxing and I fell asleep. When I woke up, oh dear, the lid was firmly shut. I didn't want to wake anyone so I just lay here relaxing and fell asleep again. Then when I woke up later, I thought bloomin 'eck because I was covered in all this frosty white stuff. Brrr, brrr, I was really shivering and cold. So I just decided to get up and go for a run around. Around the benches below was a good area to run around. So I slipped, skated, slid and whizzed about until I got some traction. Then off I went to do a few laps below. That's when I heard you shouting. But I was going too fast to stop. Maybe," he said, "all the tools could do with some exercise to warm themselves up so they're ready for work. You know… minimum fuss, maximum effort."

Arne looked and nodded. "Maybe," he said. And he started to wake the tools up because they had all gone back to sleep.

"Wakey, wakey!" Arne said, as they all started to stir.

"Morning."

"Morning."

"Morning," came the replies.

The frost was starting to slowly melt away, leaving a damp moist surface everywhere. Arne ventured further into the toolbox. As he did, it was getting warmer and more pleasant the further he got in. Deeper in the toolbox he noticed Jiggy and Sir Cular Saw, nice and warm, with a rosy glow on their cheeks. Singing and whistling while sitting on their chargers, they were all snug with a radiant glow around them. Arne set about waking the others: Tapaire, Neville, Sly, Erm, Mee, Graunch, Sawrie – and all the others in the toolbox.

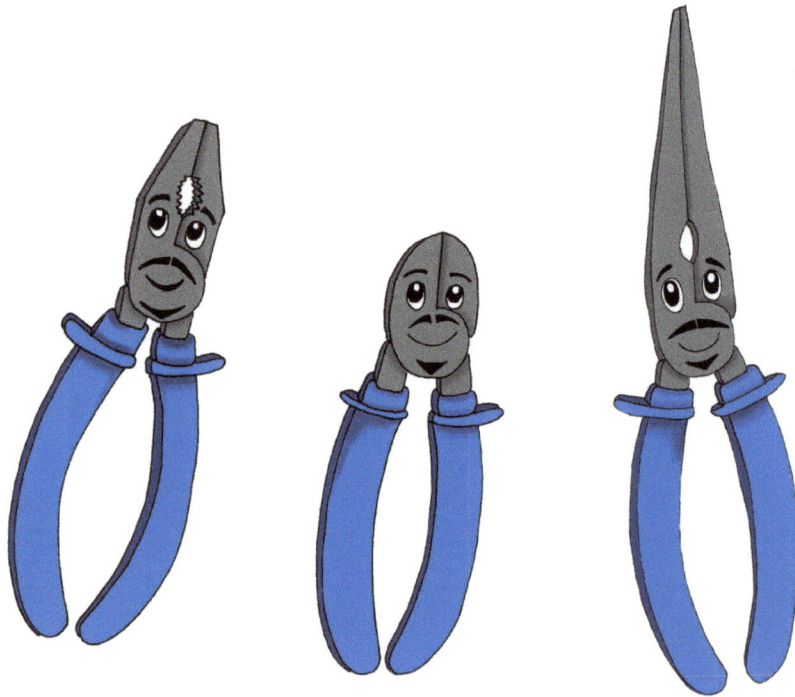

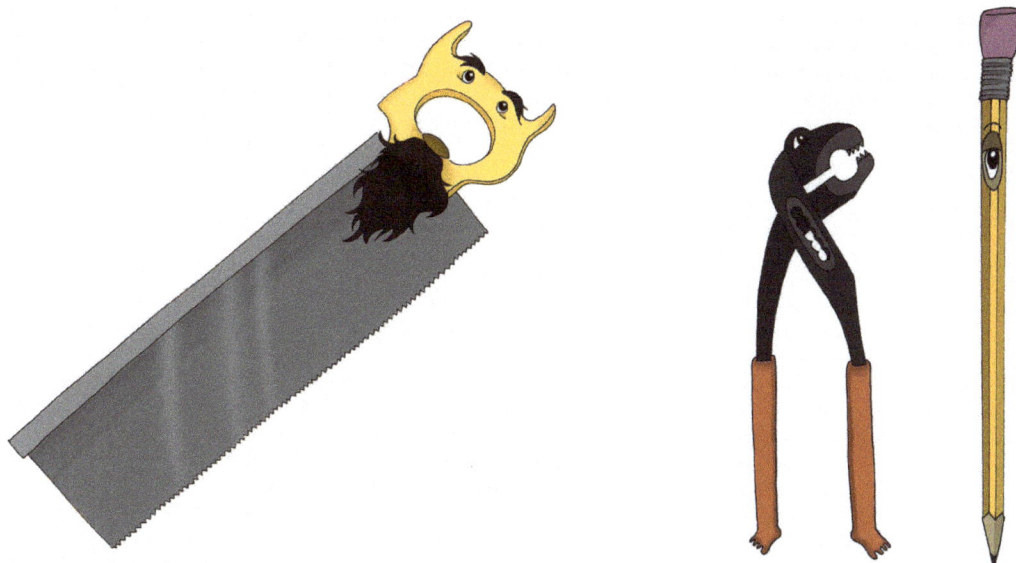

Arne shouted, "How about some exercise?" whereupon it went very quiet, with some accompanying chuckles of laughter and moaning.

But eventually the band of tools all climbed out of their box to do some warm-ups of their choice. All the tools joined in. Arne was doing some shoulder presses and squats, with loud groans of "ahh, ahh, ahh" as he lifted the bench a few times. Tapaire had run up and attached his stick lips to the top of the doorframe and was whizzing up and down on his tiny feet. Graunch was gripped around a bench support and was trapezing around and around like a circus act. Sly, Erm and Mee were traversing the bench, pulling each other up, like they were free climbing a mountain. Neville the level was balancing on a piece of tube, keeping his eyes level to avoid a headache like a tightrope walker, while Jiggy and Sir Cular just smiled and stayed in the warmth of their comfy beds in the toolbox. Sawrie, Len, and lots of other tools, were doing their own type of exercise.

Suddenly, there was a big gasp from Arne. "WHOL! What's going down?" he said, as Tapaire came bouncing and bundling past.

Bang, bing, slap, ping, blapp, blur, as he came to a stop with his eyes rolling in his head.

Arne said, "What's with the moves, Tapaire?"

He looked up trying to focus his wobbly eyes. "Wow!" he said. "I didn't see that coming."

"What happened?" said Arne.

"Hmm… basically bloomin' fell off. One moment attached to the frame, then bosh, I'm not. My sticky lips came unstuck, then timber! I was falling like a fledgling bird on their first flight from the nest. Then bang! Hit the floor, tumble and a rumble along, until I met you.

"The doorframe was a bit damp, I think," said Scribble.

"Better learn from that," said Arne.

"Yes," said Tapaire, who nodded his head, brushed himself down, checked for bruises and dents, got up, checked his hundreds of feet, and said, "Good to go."

Chapter 3

Ready for Work

The day was getting warmer and the frost and ice were disappearing. The tools were all resting and ready for work, talking amongst themselves in the toolbox. The lid was open and all was well with everyone – even Tapaire after his fall.

Later that day Leroy and his dad, Ryan, went to the basement to check the door latch to make sure it was not faulty in any way.

"Leroy," his dad said, "I have just had a big job come in from around the corner and will have to go tomorrow. Would you like to bring your toolbox?"

"Yes please, dad," Leroy answered, and he walked over to the toolbox and whispered to the tools, "Get ready, as we are going to work."

The tools inside were excited and mumbling amongst themselves in readiness for the jobs ahead. "Minimum of fuss, maximum of effort," they all said together.

Some tools were whistling, some were checking themselves over in readiness for the work ahead, but Arne was restless and fidgety and could not settle. Instead, he was pacing up and down, scratching his metal head. Then he stopped and tapped Angry's lid. Tap, tap tap.

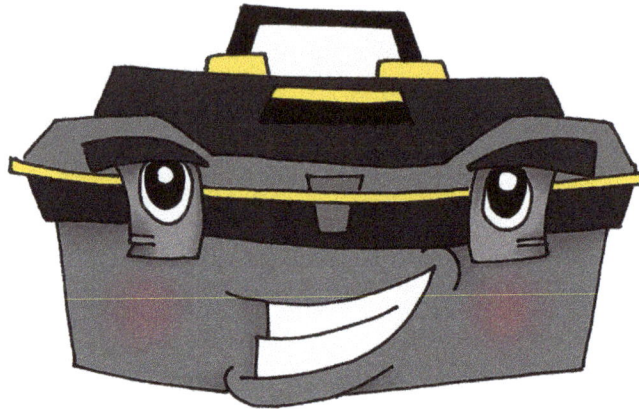

"Oh hello," said the angry toolbox.

Arne said, "I am curious."

"What?" said the toolbox.

"Well," Arne said, "I know you are happy and smiley now, but why *were* you angry?"

"Hmm…" the angry toolbox said, "let me explain. How long have we got?

"A few years ago, I was on the shelves with all the other toolboxes – the green, blue, red, orange, black, multicoloured, striped ones of all shapes and sizes – and I was a very happy smiley toolbox along with all the other toolboxes. I used to listen – or earwig, as they say – to people's conversations while they were looking at the toolboxes, and sometimes people would say bad things, which made me sad and angry. So I would shake, vibrate and sneer at them."

"But why?" said Arne.

"Well, they used to say things like, 'Cheat and you save money', or 'Buy cheap and sell expensive; they will never know'. Then they would laugh. This used to make me angry with rage, so then I would vibrate louder, snigger and shout. And this made me more angry and nasty to the other toolboxes on the shelf. This upset them. But I was upset by what these people were saying. Then I was moved to a different shelf by myself – one that nobody could see. This made me more angry, because really I was a nice toolbox, but I thought I was big and tough and I should have realised I was upsetting the other toolboxes. I was stuck all by myself, collecting lots of dust on me. It was dark and quiet on that shelf and I had no friends, and the other toolboxes said I was nasty and not nice. Hey-ho, bingo - here I am! Never the angry toolbox again"

"Oh, I see," said Arne. "So we should call you 'the nice toolbox' then?"

"Hmm… I suppose you should, but it doesn't sound the same."

Just then Arne heard a "Squeak, squeak." He looked around to see Scribble trying to squeeze himself out of the toolbox.

"Scribble," he said, "where are you off to?"

"Um," Scribble said, "I've got to go down and erase all those lines on the floor. I didn't realise I'd left all those tracks."

"Whoops," said Arne, as Scribble ventured off to clear all the lines left by his pencil lead.

"I don't want to get Leroy in trouble," he said, "as it was me running around the floor."

Once Scribble had reached the floor, he looked at Arne, did a somersault and was upside down on his eraser. Arne laughed as he looked funny with his eraser touching the floor. Scribble then started to retrace his steps, whizzing around erasing all the HB lead lines he had left on the floor. Seeing Scribble and watching him wobble about like this was making Arne chuckle and laugh hysterically, so he told the other tools, who also burst into laughter, seeing Scribble's leg and nib in the air. Eventually Scribble had erased all the lines and climbed back into the toolbox. Exhausted but happy, he had removed all the lines. The other tools gave him a loud round of applause after his epic clean.

***

Later that day Leroy collected his toolbox and placed it in his dad's truck. Clunk, as the trunk shut. Then vroom, vroom, vroom and the funny smell and vibration, which made the angry toolbox cough and splutter. The truck moved off for a short while, then stopped as Leroy collected his toolbox. The toolbox was glad that was over and the smell had gone away.

Leroy placed the toolbox next to his dad's inside the building, which looked large with lots of activity from the contractors moving around. It was nearly the end of the day and it was getting quieter within the building – and eerie as all the noise was gone. There was no movement as Ryan and Leroy walked through the house. They were looking at all the snagging work they had to put right, and putting it on a list: floors, doors, windows, pipework, painting, scratches, bumps, chips. *Phew*, Ryan thought, shaking his head in despair. *Lots to be done*. Then Ryan and Leroy left for the night, leaving the angry toolbox right there next to Ryan's toolbox.

As the toolbox was looking around in the semi-darkness, a key was heard in the door. He looked up to see Mr and Mrs Longmuir-Sturgess. This was their house that was being renovated and they had returned home from a special retirement cruise.

"Oh dear," they said, as they were not impressed with the progress. Creaky floorboards, uneven doors, and many other things. They turned and left the building with a loud bang of the front door, shaking their heads as they left.

All the while the angry toolbox was watching and observing them.

Chapter 4

Wormy the Worm

"Right then," said the angry toolbox. Then he vibrated a little and his lid slowly opened. Arne was standing there ready for work, as were all the other tools ready to get on with the tasks. The angry toolbox started to explain. "I've just seen the owners of the dwelling, but they were not impressed with the state of the work."

Arne raised an eyebrow. Then he said, "Let's see," as he raised Angry's lid and jumped to the floor. "I'm going to take a look," and he ventured off whistling a happy tune.

A while went by, then he returned, scratching his metal head. "Hmm…" he said. "Bad floor, bad door, bad everything." He looked up to see Scribble and Tapaire leaning over the toolbox and gestured to them to jump down, which they did.

Arne asked them to follow him, which they did. Arne said, "Careful, as it's moving into semi-darkness. "Watch where you tread, as there's flooring missing and joists exposed." He looked at Scribble and Tapaire and asked them, "Do you think you can walk on these exposed joists without falling or tripping?"

"Yes," they both said and nodded in agreement as they moved off along the joists. Arne, being big and strong, went first walking gently with his arms outstretched, like he was a tightrope walker in a circus. While he walked slowly, he was getting a strong whiff of something. *Hmm…* he thought, *that* stinks! He carried on further and the stink was becoming smellier. "Ha!" he said as he carried on to the door at the end of the room, thinking how springy and bouncy that was – and uneven. He shouted to Tapaire to follow, adding, "But gently."

Slowly, Tapaire started to move off along the joist, up and down over the bumps. He started to go faster, as he had lots of small feet, but he still skidded and slid and skimmed all along the joist over the humps, which had smelly flaky sawdust all along it. It was tickling his bottom and making him giggle as he eventually reached Arne by the door.

They both turned and gestured to Scribble to begin walking towards them. Scribble was really terrified and shaking – as he only has one leg and a pointy nib – *and* he was in semi-darkness. He started to make his journey, very slowly and gracefully, trying not to look down and over the edge, counting "one foot, two foot, three foot" as he moved forwards towards them.

"Pooh," he said. "What's that stink?" He could smell it as well. "That's a very stinky and strong whiff," he said, "whatever it is." As he moved on, all of a sudden, he exclaimed. "Whoa!" as he fell forwards, ending up flat on his face on the joist.

"What's the matter?" said Arne.

"Don't know," said Scribble. "I got stuck in a hole and fell over. But there are hundreds of pesky eyes looking at me," he added as he peered over the edge of the joist.

"What?" said Arne, as they disappeared without a trace.

"Eyes," said Scribble. "Scary. Lots of them. But they've gone now."

Arne was concerned, thinking Scribble was talking nonsense. So he ventured back to Scribble, who was still smelling the stinky stuff as he walked, and noticing all the small piles of sawdust on the joist.

He got back to Scribble, who was face down on the joist as he'd nearly fallen into a hole in it. Then he said, "Ah, it's blooming anobium punctatum that's made the stink. And all that dust is frass and poop around the holes."

He crouched down in front of Scribble. "Scribble," he said, "don't make a sound or move a muscle. And wait."

All of a sudden, hundreds of eyes started to slowly appear again out of the joist. Arne stood to his feet and all the eyes disappeared again. "I knew it," he said. "Anobium punctatum."

Scribble said, "What's that?"

Arne looked at Scribble and said, "Oh, it's blooming wood beetle, known as woodworm. They live in their little tunnels. Horrible stinky critters. They're what's making the stink. They poop and trump all the time. And they eat all the time – just old wood that's soft."

"What, no salad or fish or meat or big chunky fries with tomato sauce?"

"Nope," said Arne. "Just old wood. they start on one part of the wood and bore a tunnel through it – hundreds and hundreds of them. And they produce lots of frass outside their holes. It looks very much like sawdust, but it's actually *stinky poop*."

"Ah," said Scribble. "Gross. Yuck!" he added.

Arne said, "Yep, so true." Then, "Catastrophe!"

"What do you mean, Arne?" Scribble said. "Is it a problem?"

"Oh yes," said Arne. "It's past being a problem; it all needs replacing pronto."

Arne crouched down and put his hands around his head to think.

"No time to sleep," Scribble said.

"I'm not sleeping," said Arne, "but thinking."

"Well, it looked like you were sleeping," said Scribble.

Arne raised himself up and glared at Scribble sternly with an amused look. He leant towards Scribble and whispered quietly in his ear. "Listen," he said, "what we're going to do is be super quiet. I'm going to look over the edge to *my* right and you look over your edge to *your* right."

"OK," said Scribble, "but do not bang me eraser off."

Arne looked and glared and shook his head. He said, "We'll wait very quietly, then when all the critters venture out with their beady eyes, I will swing my arm and catch the blighter with the big eye, cos I reckon he's the boss."

"OK," Scribble said.

They waited for a while. Then eventually they all started to emerge from their tunnels: top, bottom, side, hundreds if not thousands of them. All was quiet. Then WHOOSH WHOOSH, Arne swung his big arm and grabbed the big-eyed dude. "Got yer!" he shouted. Then all the others disappeared again.

Arne swung his arm up in front of him, staring at his guest. "Anobium punctatum. I knew it."

The woodworm was not happy. "What did you call me?" he said.

"Anobium punctatum," Arne said.

"No, I'm not. I am a woodworm, so call me 'Wormy' if you like."

"But you don't really *look* like a worm, do you, with loads of legs, hairy everywhere, and one eye."

"I know," he said, as he was shaking with fear, "but we make holes like worms."

"We know that!" shouted Scribble. "I fell in one."

"Are you going to hurt me?"

Arne responded with a big, "No, of course not, but you are one ugly critter." He stood up, and towering above the woodworm said, "Listen, I want to talk to you about moving on from here."

Wormy said, "But we're constantly hungry and need plenty of nice wood to chew and eat – rotten old wood of course. Yum, yum."

Arne placed him in one of the many exit tunnels and stared into his big eye. Then he started to talk. "I know you're always hungry, eating and pooping at the same time, making a right old stinky smell, but this wood is going to collapse soon. I have a solution." And he started to explain:

"Outside, along the fence line of the garden, there is a dilapidated one hundred-year-old outhouse behind some vegetation with some old oak timbers."

"Ah," said wormy, "I can smell it already. Yum, yum! How far away is it?"

"It's about fifty metres," Arne said.

"How long is that?" said Wormy.

"Hmm…" Arne said, "how do *you* measure things?

"Well," said Wormy, "normally by the length of one of our bodies, which are about three centimetres long."

"Well, in that case, about one thousand and eight hundred worms."

"Oh, that far!" said Wormy. 'Well, I think that's doable."

"OK," said Arne. "Let's talk tactics then. Now, as you know, there is next to no wood left to gobble up and eat here, so you will have to vacate with all your troops. But we can help."

"How?" said Wormy.

"Well," said Arne, "we – my friend Scribble and I – will jump up and down on the joist at the same time, making it shake, rattle, vibrate and wobble. I will also ask the angry toolbox to vibrate and shake with all his might on the floor too. And all the woodworms and beetles will slide out of their tunnels and fall to the floor underneath. From there, you can venture outside.

"Wow!" said Wormy. "Sounds OK to me," as he stuck his head down a tunnel to whisper to the others. Whispering could be heard for a while as it spread through the tunnels along the joists, informing them all that they were leaving.

"OK," said Arne, "after one, two, three then."

"OK," said Wormy, as they readied themselves for their new venture.

After they'd counted, Arne and Scribble started to jump, and shake, then the angry toolbox started to vibrate with so much vigour and anger that the woodworms were falling out of their tunnels by the hundreds. All the frass on the joists was falling like snow into a massive pile on the dirt below too. All the woodworms were bouncing off the frass and into a pile at the bottom. Then they marched two by two along a gully, like all the animals going to Noah's ark, singing 'hi ho, hi ho' as they left.

Eventually all the woodworms were gone. Arne looked down to see them marching away to the outside. The big-eyed boss worm turned and waved and shouted, "Who called me an 'anobium punctatum'?"

"Don't know," said Arne, "Some insectarian, I believe."

"A what?" said Wormy.

"Just some boffin who gives silly names to things."

"Oh thanks," he said as he left.

Chapter 5

Work to Be Done

Now all the woodworms were gone, Arne walked along the joists and jumped up and down. It was bouncy and creaking.

"We'll have to replace all these joists."

"What if they come back?" said Scribble.

"They won't," said Arne, "as we're going to fit nice new wood."

"They hate new wood." But where, this wood coming from, said scribble.

"Well," said Arne, "firstly it comes from special places where there is too much wood. And it is cut down by special people with machines. Then it is inspected and given a kind of haircut on the outside. It's then written on so we know when and where it comes from. Then it's cut into special lengths the same size as these, and finally sprayed in a very nasty juice that makes critters very sick."

"Oh," said Scribble.

Just then Tapaire arrived back. "What have you been up to?" he asked.

"It's a long story," said Arne. "We had to get rid of all the anobium punctatum."

"What's that?" said Tapaire.

"Woodworm," said Arne.

"Didn't look like worms to me," said Scribble. "Too many legs."

"Yes, but they are called that – or wood beetles."

"Oh, them blooming beasts," said Tapaire.

Arne carried on explaining to Scribble, "They don't like new wood because it's too tough, not tasty enough and got that horrible juice on it which makes their teeth fall out and go blunt. So we can be assured it will be safe for many years to come, and they will be more than happy with that old dilapidated shed."

It was getting dark and they started to venture along the joists, Arne, Tapaire, then Scribble. Suddenly, they heard a shout. "Oh no! Ah… ah… ah… ah…" getting quieter until nothing. Scribble had toppled over the edge. Over and over he tumbled into the abyss, ending upright nib first stuck in the moist dirt in complete darkness. Scribble was scared. It was eerie, and he was stuck fast in the dirt.

Arne and Tapaire walked back, both calling his name, but he was nowhere to be seen. Their worst nightmare was coming true. "He's fallen over," they said, as they moved along the joist shouting, "Scribble, Scribble."

Eventually, Scribble responded. "I'm down here," he said in the dark, stuck in the dirt.

Arne and Tapaire looked over the edge, but it was pitch black and felt very damp and eerie. They couldn't see him in the darkness below.

Meanwhile, Scribble tried to wobble and push to release himself. "Ah… ah… ah…" he gasped, as he pushed with all his might to free himself from the moist damp dirt many times until his little arms were worn out. He was exhausted and stuck fast.

***

As he rested to think out his next plan, he heard a kind of slither in the darkness, then he felt a sticky breath on his neck. *Whoa*, Scribble thought, then said out loud, "What is that?"

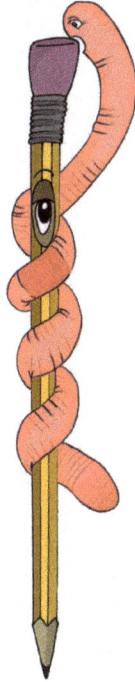

Suddenly there was a noise, then a voice said, "Who are you, and what do you want?" as a big eye popped up very close in front of Scribble, inspecting him up and down.

Scribble said, "I'm sorry, but I just fell from up there: I tumbled over and over until I ended up in this dirt."

"But this is my patch," said the voice, "and me and my family live down here. And we don't like invaders."

Scribble apologised again and said, "I'm not an invader, just a passer-by who fell down here. It was an accident and I don't mean any harm to you – or anyone."

"Hmm…" he said.

Scribble then asked, "What are you?"

"I am a worm," he said. "A long slithery stretchy earthworm, and I live in the earth and come out now and then for fresh air and food."

As he said this, Scribble tensed up because the worm had started to wrap himself around Scribble and was giving him a large slurpy lick up and down.

"No," said Scribble, as the lick made him ticklish.

"Hmm…" said the worm, "bit stiff and shiny, and no taste."

"Yes," said Scribble. "I am not edible."

All of a sudden, the worm opened his mouth and Scribble's eraser disappeared into it. He tried to chew it, lick it, bite it, then released it. "Yuck, yuck!" the worm said.

"I told you," said Scribble. "I am not food."

"Horrible," said the worm. "Not tasty at all."

"No," replied Scribble. "Just as I told you."

"Now," Scribble said, "if you are nice, could you help me get out of this earth, then I will disappear and you will never see me again."

"OK," said the worm. "What can I do?"

Scribble said, "Can you wrap yourself around my waist, like you just did, but don't lick or bite."

"OK," said the worm. And he wrapped himself around Scribble.

Scribble said, "When I push, can you pull, and we'll see if I can move?"

"OK," said the worm."

"After three," said Scribble. "One, two, three… Ah, ah, oh, oh, eh, eh, darn, darn!"

Just then, Scribble heard his voice being called. It was getting louder every time. But, he was having no luck. He was still stuck fast in the dirt. The shouting got louder by the second, and he looked up into the darkness to see Tapaire appearing from nowhere.

"Hello," said Tapaire. "What happened to you?"

"I just tripped and, whoops, ended up here. Thought I was a goner."

"Oh dear," said Tapaire. "Let's get you out of here."

All of a sudden, Tapaire shouted, "What's that?"

"Oh," said Scribble, "that's my friend the worm who's been trying to help me."

"OK," said Tapaire. "He's only got one eye like you, Scribble."

"Yes," said Scribble, "but he only needs one down here, he said."

Tapaire said, "I've managed to hook my lips and teeth on the joist and Arne is up there with his foot on them, so we haven't got long. And I managed to abseil down to collect you. Then he asked the worm, "Are you a proper worm, or a worm that's a beetle?"

"No," said the worm. "I'm a proper slithery slimy moist stretchy earthworm. But why do you ask?"

"Well," said Tapaire, "up at the top, there are beetles that *call* themselves worms, but they have lots of hairy legs."

"No," said the worm. "They're not proper worms; they're fake worms."

Tapaire looked at the proper earthworm. "Where do you live?"

"Here," he said, "in the earth."

"Don't go out much then?" said Tapaire.

"No, don't need to," came the reply.

Tapaire then introduced himself to the friendly worm. "My name is Tapaire and I am Scribble's friend. Pleased to meet you."

"Likewise," said the worm.

Tapaire said to the worm, "If you stay wrapped around Scribble, can you hook your tail end around that dangly piece of wood?"

Then to Scribble, he instructed, "Scribble, you hold on to me and I'll put all my dangly feet onto you, then we'll attempt to free you. On the count of three… here we go… one, two, three, lift."

"Ah, eh, hmm… ah, eh, eh." All of a sudden, Scribble started to become free from the earth and began to rise up into the darkness. The worm uncoiled himself from Scribble as they rose up in the darkness. Scribble looked down and thanked the worm for his help; he slithered back along the floor to his home.

Tapaire and Scribble were rising slowly in the darkness until they reached the joist, whereupon Arne reached down and grabbed Scribble by his eraser rim, then yanked him to safety.

Arne said, "His hand was covered in goo. It was all sticky and slimy."

"Oh yes," said Scribble. "My friend, Wormy, tried to eat me. He put his slimy saliva all over my eraser."

"Yuck!" said Arne. "You'd better clean yourself up."

Tapaire was also now on the joist.

Arne asked, "Are you in good shape and ready for work?"

They both nodded and moved along the joist slowly, avoiding all the exit tunnels and all the mounds of frass. The wood was rotten and soft, but they all made it over to the door into the next room. The room where they sat down to discuss which job to do first had broken skirting boards.

Arne sat up and asked Tapaire to go back to the angry toolbox and get Neville the level, Lever Len, Sir Cular saw, and Jiggy to assist with the next stage.

Chapter 6

Finding the Wood

A while later they all arrived back safely. Arne wanted to do the dodgy skirting boards but knew that the joists were more important, as they were rotten. They needed new wood.

Arne scratched his metal head, then his eyes lit up with glee. "I know," he said, "when we came into the house the first time, I noticed at the end of the yard, there was a big pile of new wood, which was going to be used elsewhere. It was located past the old dilapidated shed." Then he got up and asked Lever Len and Scribble to join him.

Off they ventured out into the semi-darkness, up and down over obstacles, passing a wheelbarrow, a greenhouse for plants, and the old dilapidated shed where all the woodworms were. Onwards towards a hill on the path that they were following. Arne was in front and began to climb the hill, which was all covered in mud. As he did, the hill, or mound, started to get all prickly and sharp on his feet. Lever Len was next and he was also experiencing extreme prickliness as he walked. "Oh, ooh, ah," he said. "Strange hill," he added as he finally got to the other side.

Then Scribble started to venture over the hill. All of a sudden, there was a loud shout from the hill. "Ouch, ouch, ouch," came the noise very loudly. And the hill started to move gently, like a small earthquake. Scribble did no more.

He bolted up and over the top and down the other side. All the while, the hill was making "ohm, ahh, ouch" sounds until Scribble reached the other side and jumped onto the path, where Arne and Lever Len were waiting. They all stared at each other with bewilderment.

All of a sudden, a loud shout was heard. "Oh, oh, you lot."

Arne, Len and Scribble all started to turn very slowly as a very moist wet nose came sniffing and snuffling in the undergrowth until it was nose to nose with Arne.

The voice said, "Do you mind. You woke me up and were hurting my back. Especially the one with the pointy foot."

Arne was almost bent backwards by the nose pushing him. "Scary!" said Arne. "But who are you? We thought you were a hill."

"A hill?" he hissed. "I am a hedgehog. And I was in a state of hibernation, very happy in the darkness in this vegetation."

"Sorry," voiced Arne. "We didn't mean to disturb you; we were just on our way to retrieve some wood at the bottom of the yard." He then asked, "What's 'hibernating'?"

"Oh," said the voice, "it's when I go to sleep when it's cold. And I just rest and sleep all the time for a few months."

"Do you not eat?" asked Lever Len.

"No," said Hedgy the hog. I eat enough before I sleep, like a big grizzly bear."

"Do you poop?" said Scribble.

"Don't think so," said Hedgy the hog.

"Blimey! Sounds good if you don't poop for ages," said Scribble. "But do you not get bellyache and full of wind?"

Arne looked at the hedgehog and said, "I've never seen you before."

"Hedgy said, "That's because I'm not from around here. I came from Europe originally. I came over on a big ship. When it docked, the big box I was in, which was full of vegetables, went to a ranch down the road with me in it. When it was opened, and I was defrosted, I bolted like an Olympic runner out over the fields into the woods and into this lovely garden. And I've been here ever since that day – about two years ago."

"Gorblimey!" said Scribble. "Excuse me, but you don't *look* as if you can bolt like an Olympic runner."

"Well, maybe not, but I ran and was on top of a hill, then I rolled up like a prickly ball and trundled down the hill superfast. Once at the bottom, I stopped and walked into this garden. And here I am," Hedgy said. He looked at Arne, Len, Scribble, and then pleaded, "Please don't tell anyone I'm here, as I'm no danger to the land or the environment or other species." Then he asked, "Where are you off to?"

We're going to inspect and collect some wood at the end of the garden."

"Oh," said Hedgy. "I'll be here when you return."

They all moved on and found the pile of timber covered up where it should be. They inspected it and Arne said, "Perfect! It has a date stamp and it's marked up."

"Lever Len said, "Does it matter if it's written on or not?"

Arne replied, "Oh yes, as that tells you exactly where, and what, and exactly how it got here, and how it was felled. He smelt the timber and stated, "Perfect! And freshly cut." Then he asked Lever Len to lie flat, whereupon he started to pile the timber on top of him until Len could carry no more.

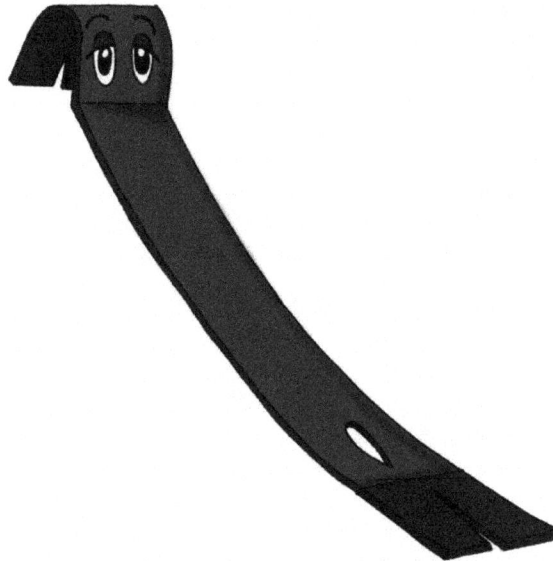

"Enough," he said, as his belly was touching the floor. He could carry no more.

They started to make their way back slowly. Len was huffing and puffing and scraping his belly along the floor. Eventually, Arne lifted a couple of lengths to ease the weight and burden on him.

"Thanks," said Len, as they moved back towards Hedgy the hog. Eventually they reached him.

"Hello," said Arne. "Is it OK for us to venture back over you?"

"Hmm…" said Hedgy. "Could you run, as that would help me, *and* stop you getting prickly feet."

Arne said, "We can try."

But Len shook his head. "I don't think so," he said. "Not with all this weight."

Scribble looked and said, "OK, I'll give it a go and run up and over as fast as I can."

Arne followed quickly up and over to the other side, but unfortunately, Len was just too heavy carrying so much weight, and he was even slower than before.

"Bloomin' 'eck," said Hedgy as Len started to venture across.

"Sorry," said Len, huffing and puffing as he went. Then he chuckled and giggled because his belly was prickled and tickled as he crossed. Eventually, he reached the other side.

"Bloomin' marvellous!" said Hedgy. "Glad that's over."

Arne, Len and Scribble thanked him and moved on back to the house. It was getting lighter by the minute; the contractors would soon be back. They started to move quicker as daylight was appearing on the horizon. They were fast approaching the dilapidated old shed. And as they did, they started to smell the rotten stink again. As they smelt it, they looked over to see Woody and all the other worms lying down on the old wood, with the biggest massive bellies.

Arne stopped. "Phew! That stinks," he said.

"Yep," came the reply from Woody. "Sorry," he added. "Belly rot," as all the worms were resting outside on the old wood. "Lovely stuff, this wood," he added. "You can see that, can't you?" he said, pointing at the others as they all tapped their big full fat bellies. Tap, tap, tap. Slap, slap. Solid. Too fat to move, they lay still with all the frass and sawdust alongside them.

"Looks like it was tasty," said Arne.

"*Really* tasty," they said, as they made lots of moans and loud trumping noises. "Never tasted anything so good before." And they belched and burped while lying lazily in the early dawn light.

Arne, holding his nose, moved on away from the stinky woodworms. With Scribble and Len not far behind, they moved towards the house. As they got nearer, the smell was disappearing. They entered the house where the bad joists were.

Lever Len was by now totally worn out from his epic trip. He put the wood down with a sigh of relief while looking at his very sore belly. And he went to meet the other tools. It was now getting light, so they all decided to return to the angry toolbox to relax and recuperate and carry on that evening.

Chapter 7

Work to Be Done

The evening was upon them and the contractors were all leaving. Leroy and his dad, Ryan, were also leaving for the night. So once it was quiet, Arne gently lifted the lid of the toolbox. "Alright?" Arne said.

The toolbox said, "Yep."

"Just checking if the coast is clear."

It was, so Arne lifted the toolbox lid until it was open. He stood up and gestured to the others, who all sat up, then got up. Arne stood up and looked over to ask Scribble, Lever Len, Sir Cular saw, Neville the level, Jiggy and Tapaire de Rule to assist with the work ahead.

"We've got to replace the faulty floor joists tonight with the ones we got this morning," Arne said.

"OK," came the reply as they moved to the infested worn joists, which still smelt bad from all the ejected frass around the tunnels.

Scribble stood up and asked Arne, "This frass, or sawdust, that is produced by those woodies... How...? said Scribble.

Arne responded, "Frass," he said, "or frassssssse, basically goes in via their face and out of their, er, oh, hmm... backside."

"Oh," said Scribble. "What, continuously?"

"Yep," said Arne. "Non-stop."

"What? Eat and poop at the same time? Yuck!" said Scribble. He scratched his head in bewilderment as they all moved into the corner to carry out the work ahead.

They all knew their task and started to proceed. Tapaire attached himself by his sticky lips, lowering himself down, swinging like a pendulum to and fro like a mountain climber traversing a crevasse, eventually attaching himself to the worn joist at a forty-five degree angle. Scribble slid down the tape, scribing a line as he went on all the joists that needed replacing for Sir Cular to cut. Sir Cular got into position, attaching his safety line to the joist, and cut them one by one. The worn joists fell to the floor. He was like a lumberjack felling trees. All the infected worn rotten wood was cut away. Sir Cular was pleased with his work and returned to the top until he was required again.

Arne collected the new wood, Tapaire measured, and Sir Cular cut the new wood to its required angle on all the pieces required. Arne thanked them for their work, and proceeded to carefully lift each new piece of wood into place, with a final clump from his big head – bang – until the final piece was fitted.

"A perfect fit!" he said as he stood up and walked gently along, stamping with his feet as he collected some clout nails to secure the joists into place, making them safe and secure, ready for the new floor to be laid down. They all moved off into the next room, where they had a small rest while talking and telling stories. Arne stood up, looked at the next job and declared, "All the skirting board must come off, as it's been fitted incorrectly; it's all out of alignment."

Arne approached the first piece around the room and looked at its imposing length while deciding on a plan of attack. "Lever Len, Tapaire, Scribble and Jiggy, you'll start the work," he said. Then he grabbed the first length and started to bend it outwards.

Lever Len wedged himself between the wall and the board and started to heave and push with Arne. It creaked and pinged as it started to release from the wall. Then with a final BANG it was off. The boards were released from the walls, and Arne sat down with his back to the removed boards that were facing all the other tools. As he did this, he noticed Lever Len, who was walking very slowly backwards away from him. *Strange*, thought Arne. As he looked around, Scribble and Tapaire and Jiggy were also walking slowly away from Arne with a strange look on their faces.

As Len took another step back, he said, "Arne, do you know anyone with a very moist pink nose?"

"Nope," said Arne.

Then Scribble said, "Arne, do you know anyone with a long scaly tail?"

"Nope," said Arne.

As they all took another step backwards Jiggy said, "Arne, do you know anyone with big ears that look like dried grapes?"

"No," said Arne.

Once again they took a step backwards and Tapaire said, "Arne, do you know anyone with small beady eyes and enormous whiskers?"

Once again Arne said, "No." Then suddenly, all the tools turned around and scarpered behind the door.

"Strange," said Arne as he sat there in bewilderment. A moment later, Arne felt a hot sticky breath behind him, which was accompanied by a squeaky noise. *Oh dear*, he thought as he turned around slowly. "Whoah, whoah," Arne stuttered as he stood in fear for a second facing forwards while feeling the hot sticky breath on his face.

All of a sudden a voice said, "What are you doing in my house?"

Arne, shaking with fear, bent backwards with a big pink moist nose against his chest. There were also two big ears and wide whiskers.

"Mickey he shouted.

"Mickey?" said the voice. "I'm not a Mickey, I'm a dormouse. I've lived here with my family for years and you've taken away the door to my house."

"Uh yes," said Arne, "but there is a reason. It's because it's not fitted correctly and we are putting things right."

"Why in *my* house?" the mouse said. "We run all over the house from room to room, up walls, hole to hole, beam to beam, crack to crack, looking for any food. Got any cheese?" he added.

"No," replied Arne. "I've got no cheese."

"What about peanut butter?" said the mouse.

"No," said Arne. "No cheese or peanut butter." Then he asked, "Is that all you eat then?"

"No," said the mouse, "but it's very tasty and nice. It's what those nasty people put on little traps to try and hurt us, but we're too clever for them and do not eat it. But it smells lovely."

Arne looked at the mouse and said, "No, nothing for you to eat. Sorry."

"Mmm…" said the mouse sadly, with a tear in his eye.

"What's the matter?" said Arne.

"Well," said the mouse, "you see sometimes, we find some lovely smelling food, but it's put down by a person in a white coat and hat – not to feed us, but to make us very ill."

"Oh yes," said Arne, "he's the mouse and rat catcher."

"Yes, nasty man," said the mouse. "Doesn't like us," said the mouse. "Don't know why."

Arne voiced, "But you live in someone's house and you shouldn't be here. You chew all the wood, you make holes everywhere, you run around in the dark, you chomp on the electrical cables and all the lights go out, *and*… you leave loads of poo everywhere."

"Yes," said the mouse, "but you gotta poo. If you eat, you gotta poo." He was sniffling all over Arne, then looked at him and asked again, "You *sure* you've got no cheese?"

Arne said, "No, but look, I know you love to be inside in the warm this time of year. What if I show you a place you can live near here which will be warm all the time – and comfy – *and* you might be happy about where it is."

"Where is it then?" said the mouse.

"Come with me," said Arne, and off they went out of the room along the joists until Arne stopped. "Down there," he said, pointing.

"What's that?" said the mouse.

"It's a big pile of soft comfy frass – a very deep pile, so deep and so soft you can get lost in it.

"Mmm…" said the mouse. "Is this a trick?"

"No," said Arne, "I'm trying to help you."

The mouse looked down into the unknown with his small beady eyes focussed on the massive pile of frass. "Mmm…" he said. "It does look good." Then he added, "Nothing ventured, nothing gained," as he took a leap of faith into the darkness, hoping for a soft landing.

The mouse landed very softly on the frass, bouncing and tumbling and toppling in every direction, running in and out. "Wow!" came his reply, with a big mousy grin on his face as he burrowed in and out without any restrictions. "Lovely!" he said as he rested flat out on top of the frass. "Bit stinky though," he added while giggling with glee.

He looked up at Arne. "Thanks," he said. "This is fantastic!" as he somersaulted all over the frass. He was happy with this for his family home. He was so happy and ecstatic he skimmed up the wall and back to get his family straight away.

A short while later he appeared again with Mrs Mouse, little boy mouse and little baby girl mouse. They all launched themselves into the big furry soft pile of frass. They were scooting all over the place in and out as happy as can be, eventually stopping and resting with big smiles on their faces. "Thank you," they all said and moved off to make their new home in the middle of it.

Arne looked and nodded, and made his way back to the other room, looking for the others. He could see Lever Len hiding behind some removed wood. He was shaking a little.

"Has it gone?" said Len.

"Yes, it's gone," said Arne. "Found the family a new home."

"Phew!" said Len. "I'm pleased about that," as he scrambled out from behind the pile of wood.

Scribble was hiding in a hole in the wall that he'd managed to slide himself into. Tapaire was on the doorframe. Jiggy and Sir Cular were hiding under a box, which was vibrating on the floor due to them shaking with fear.

"Stop!" said Arne as they all started to come out. Eventually they were all back together.

They all began to assist in the replacement of the wooden pieces, Neville balancing on top saying, "Left, right, up, down"; Arne bashing in some nails; Tapaire making sure all was cut correctly and to the correct length. After a while, all the pieces were fitted. Neville balanced himself on each one, checking they were all straight and not wonky. This made him happy, with no wonky eyes or headache.

They all rested and looked at the work they had done. And they were really happy with the outcome: no bodges, no shoddy workmanship, just a good job with… minimum of fuss and maximum of effort. As they did this, Scribble said, "On our journey today, we have met Woody the worm, Hedgy the hog, Wiggly the worm, and Mickey the mouse. And guess what… they are all happy where they are now with our help.

"You're correct," said Arne. "All's well that ends well."

Chapter 8

The Last Task

The toolbox and tools had carried out so many jobs and completed them to a great standard. But the last and final job would be tricky, they thought, as they all looked up at the door and gave it a long stare.

"Bloomin' 'eck," said Scribble.

Tapaire said, "No problem."

Arne gulped and said, "We will prevail," as they started to talk tactics. He began to push the door open a little. Creak, crack, squeak – as it was completely incorrectly fitted: hinges bent, door not level, a bit of a task. As they looked up at the three hinges fitted to the door, Arne said, "Ahh… screws… and we need some drivers."

"Drivers," they all said.

"Yep," said Arne, "screwdrivers to remove the screws."

All the other tools looked at each other with concerned looks, shrugged their shoulders, and pulled funny faces as Arne asked, "Are there any drivers in Angry?"

Once again there was a strange look from them all and a reply of, "We don't know."

Arne said, "OK then," as he looked at Scribble and asked, "Scribble, could you go back to the toolbox, look inside and ask if there are any screwdrivers."

Scribble ventured back, climbed into the toolbox asked him, "Do we have any screwdrivers?"

To which the angry toolbox replied, "I have no idea, but Leroy would know."

But Leroy was not there. Scribble started to climb down in the darkness asking, "Are there any screwdrivers here?" Further down he went, getting darker as he did, until he reached Jiggy and Sir Cular's charger. "OK," he said, "there is a light on their charger." And he turned it on to lots of moans and groans from below. "Sorry," he said as he went from shelf to shelf, looking and asking for screwdrivers.

As he did, he lifted up covers, firstly a camouflage cover, from which came, "Hello. Sergeant Tack, and this is my army of tacks."

"Thanks," said Scribble, "but we need some screwdrivers at this time."

As he replaced the cover, Sergeant Tack saluted. Scribble moved along to another cover alongside the tacks.

He started to ruffle the cover, when suddenly, a head popped out from below. "Mr Clout at your service," a voice said. "And these are my army of clout nails, ready for work."

"OK," said Scribble, "thanks, but I'm looking for screwdrivers."

"OK," said Mr Clout, but if you need some fixings, here we are," as the cover went back on them.

Scribble moved further on into the toolbox. He burrowed further down until he found a cover with a zip on it. He started to unfasten it, but as he did this, it began to zip up again. Scribble undid it once more, and again it started to close up. So he knocked on the cover and said, "Excuse me."

"Yes," came the reply.

"Can I help you?"

Scribble said, "Maybe," and then asked if they were screwdrivers.

"Yes, we are," came the reply.

"Wonderful!" he said. "My name is Scribble and we need some help."

"Who does?" said the screwdriver.

Scribble said, "Arne the club hammer does. Do you know him?"

"Hmm…" said the screwdriver, "is he tall with a square head, a shiny hickory shaft, big shoulders, strong and from Austria?"

"Yes," said Scribble.

"No, don't know him," came the reply, then started to close the zip on the cover.

"Wait," said Scribble as he jumped on the zip. We need your help," whereupon the zip stopped and a head popped back out.

The screwdriver was happy and warm in his bed, not doing anything. All of a sudden three more heads appeared from under the cover.

"Hello," said Scribble as they looked out.

Mrs Screwdriver said, "What can we help you with, as it's quite nice and cosy in here and we've not been out for a while. But we could do with some exercise, I suppose."

Scribble said, "We need some help with some door hinges – to remove the screws in them."

"Ah," said Mrs Screwdriver, "we can help as we have all types of tips to change into: slotted, Hexagon, Phillips, Torx, Pozidriv and a few other odd ball tips. We'll bring them along."

They all ventured out and climbed up to the top of the toolbox to the outside, to meet Arne and the other tools. Carefully scurrying along the new wooded joists, without falling off or into the space below, they could hear lots of laughter from below.

"Yes," said Scribble. "Arne found a nice new home for a Micky mouse and his family and they love where they're living in their new home."

Eventually the family of screwdrivers reached Arne and the other tools.

"We understand you need some help," said the screwdrivers.

Arne welcomed the screwdrivers and thanked them for coming to help "Yes, we sure do," said Arne. "We must remove the screws in the door hinges."

The family of screwdrivers looked and Mummy Driver said, "Pozidriv… this one's for me," as she scurried in her bag for the correct tip. "OK, done," she said as she slipped on the correct screwdriver tip. Then off she went scurrying up the doorframe, getting herself located in the first hinge screw. Then she began rotating backwards and forwards until the screw started to undo, faster and faster, twisting in the same direction until it was out. She was removing all the other screws while singing, "Come on, everybody, let's do the twist," while her family laughed and giggled.

Eventually all the screws were removed. Arne, Scribble, Lever Len, and Tapaire, who had all been supporting the door, dropped it to the floor with a "clump!" Then they removed it and took it away so they could repair it.

The tools looked at the door. It required a slither of wood taken off its top and side. Arne asked Sir Cular to assist with the task. Sir Cular looked at the door laid flat in order to access the work, then he sat by the door edge, earphones on, glasses on, and off he went whizzing up the door edge to remove a slither of wood, then along the top to remove another piece. Completely covered in sawdust, Arne was happy with the job.

Another good job carried out by the tools! Arne and the other tools lifted the door back into position as Mummy Driver scurried up the door and replaced all the screws, singing, "Let's twist again, like we did last summer" as all the screws were put back in the hinges.

"Job done!" said Arne, happy with the work. The door was now back in place and closing perfectly.

Just then, Leroy was heard to come into the room. "Ryan," Leroy's dad said, "we'll have to leave soon, so make sure you have all your tools."

Arne looked at all the tools and said, "Looks like we have to go."

So they gently started to walk back along the joists – screwdrivers, Jiggy, Sir Cular, Tapaire, Lever Len, Neville the level, Arne, then finally Scribble, all making their way back to the toolbox. The weather outside was wet and stormy, like a hurricane, with wind and black skies and lots of thunder and lightning. All the tools gradually reached the toolbox, climbed in and got settled inside, Arne and Scribble being the last to arrive. Arne was lucky because as he climbed in the toolbox, the lid was slammed shut by Leroy, who had to get himself and the toolbox in the trunk of the truck, but it was dark inside the toolbox. And Arne knew that Scribble was not inside. He was quite frantic and started to shove the lid off the toolbox, but it was no use, he couldn't open it up.

He was upset and shouted to the angry toolbox. "Angry!"

"Yes," came the reply from the toolbox.

"Scribble's not here," he said to him.

Suddenly, the toolbox rocked from side to side as it was being lifted and carried to Ryan's truck. It was placed on the tailgate. Then, as the toolbox was getting battered with rain and thunder, it managed to open its hinges to allow Arne to look outside. He looked over the edge and could see Scribble running towards the toolbox, all the while being battered and bruised by the wind and the rain. He kept falling over, and then getting up again as he made his way nearer each time to the truck.

Arne was shouting, "Come on, Scribble."

But the rain was horrendous. Scribble was holding onto plants and trees on the way to the truck.

"Come on," said Arne. "You can make it. Remember: 'minimum of fuss, maximum of effort. MINIMUM OF FUSS, MAXIMUM OF EFFORT! Scribble was getting exhausted from being battered by the wind and rain, but he just managed to reach the truck's tailgate. Grabbing onto it for his life, shocked, wet, cold, and worn out, he was still not safe.

The wind was hurricane force. Scribble managed to climb a nearby wall to gain access to the tailgate. Launching himself onto it, he landed on the edge, stumbling, and still being blasted by the storm. Arne was looking out of the toolbox with his outstretched arm, muscles bulging, enticing Scribble to grab hold.

All of a sudden, there was a jerk as the truck started to move. Arne grabbed the toolbox as it shook and vibrated with the movement, and he glanced towards Scribble. "Oh no!" came a shout. Scribble had been on the tailgate edge, but his hands were now flailing in the air as he tumbled backwards off the truck, landing on a tree branch, then cascading down the road into the gutter where torrential rain had caused a fast-flowing river.

Scribble looked up towards Arne as Arne looked down towards Scribble.

Scribble was locked on fast to a certain tree branch as it started to pass the truck. He looked up towards Arne with a defiant gesture of one raised arm, which punched the air. "Arne, I'll be back. I'll be back," he shouted.

Arne looked over, with tears in his eyes. "Scribbs, Scribbs, we'll find you. We *will* find you," he shouted back as the truck moved away from the driveway.

The toolbox had closed to the weather outside. There were tears in the eyes of all those who had watched the toolbox as it moved gently away. With no words from within, there was a stunned silence from all the tools, who were devastated at the loss of their friend. As they moved further away, they knew that Scribble was cascading further down the road. Nowhere was he to be seen now. They knew Scribble was lost, but they vowed to find him, no matter where, what or when. With the minimum of fuss and the maximum of effort, they promised to find him. Shocked and silenced, the truck moved back to the house, with all inside the toolbox knowing they would find and rescue Scribble.

THE END

www.ingramcontent.com/pod-product-compliance
Lightning Source LLC
LaVergne TN
LVHW070838080426
835510LV00030B/3443

9 781836 150725